Principles of Football

by coach Enrico Pomarico

Principles of Football • © 2020 Enrico Pomarico

Welcome to this brief guide to football positions, tactics and strategies.

Everyone in a team is important just like many pieces of a jigsaw puzzle that couldn't be completed if just one piece went missing.

All players can contribute to achieve the objectives even by playing only 5 minutes or less, or saying the right words in the changing room, or simply leading by example: working hard, being disciplined, professional and respectful in every situation.

In the following pages we are going to explore all the aspects of each position for young players to learn more about their roles and perhaps find interest in trying a different position.
Look out for the extra "Tactical Input" pages at the end of each section!

Table of contents

Tactical input

- Goalkeeper out of possession   Page 14
- Goalkeeper in possession   Page 16
- The Offside   Page 26
- "La Diagonale"   Page 36
- Compactness   Page 52
- Crossing zones   Page 60
- Striker's tricks   Page 68
- Manager's strategies   Page 76
- Technical language   Page 80

Manager
Page 70

Principles of Football • © 2020 Enrico Pomarico

Goalkeeper
Page 6

Centre-back
Page 18

Full-backs
Page 30

Central midfielders
Page 38

Wingers
Page 54

Striker
Page 62

Principles of Football • © 2020 Enrico Pomarico

Goalkeeper

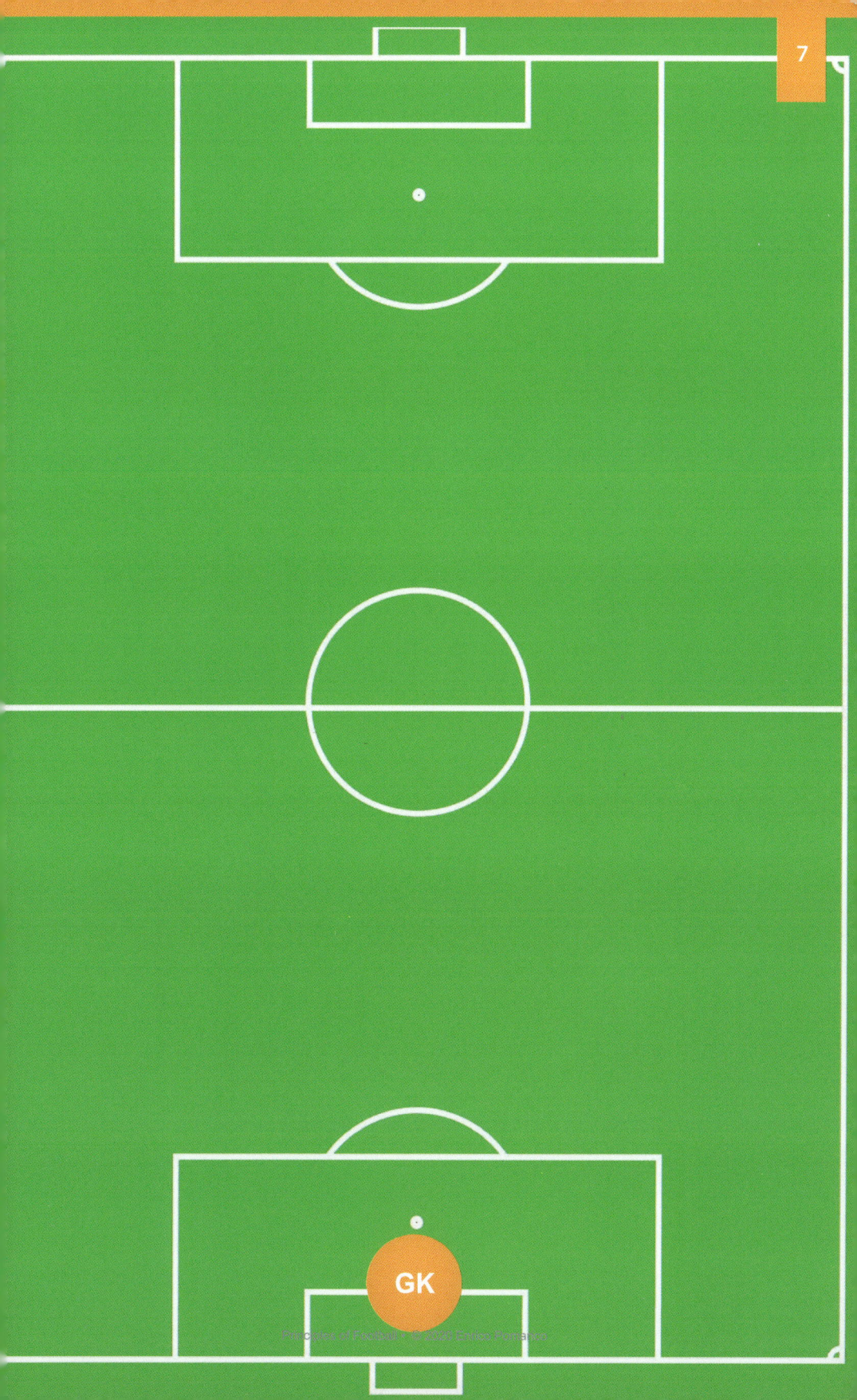

8

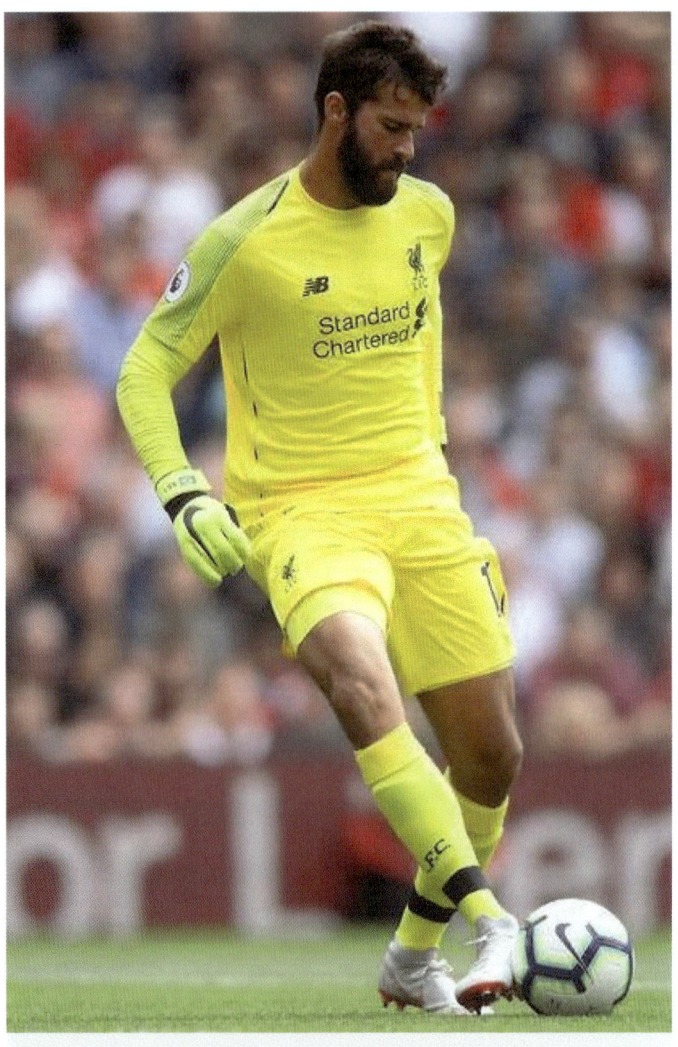

Alisson Becker, Brazil

Goalkeeper

The Goalkeeper, often shortened to keeper or goalie, is the most specialized position in football, in fact the GK is mostly training separately.

GK (usually the player wearing the no. 1) is a role of great responsibility and sacrifice.

They have a major role in the team; whilst saving doesn't score points, every little mistake might cost very heavily.

In 1v1 situations the technical manual says "to try occupying as much space as possible to protect the goal" which means that the GK is accepting the idea of being hit by powerful shots in their face, belly, underbelly and possibly breaking fingers.

In modern football the Goalkeeper is not only required to be a **Shot Stopper** but to be also **Sweeper Keeper**.

Since 1992 the GK is not allowed to handle a back pass by a teammate, rule made to avoid time waste.

In more recent times the top teams have begun playing "from the back" in possession and to bring "high pressure" out of possession forcing the GK to become instrumental to the new style of play. Therefore the GK needs to be also "good with the feet" which is an aspect of their training that was neglected for decades.

Ter Stegen, Germany

Often the captain of the team, the GK is always a leading figure in the changing room and on the pitch. Loud and determined the GK directs the defense and motivates the team.
In history there has been also GKs scoring goals, specialised in taking penalties and free kicks.

It's common to see the Goalkeeper going up in the opponent's box for a corner on the last action when the team desperately needs a goal and yes, it has happened that the Goalkeeper was in the right place at the right time and saved the day!

Hope Solo, USA

Ederson, Brazil

Main tasks:

- Blocking shots
- Exiting on crosses and through passes
- Organising the defense
- Organising the wall on set pieces
- Goal kicks, long or short passing
- Supporting the teammates in possession
- Motivating the teammates on and off the pitch

Attributes required:

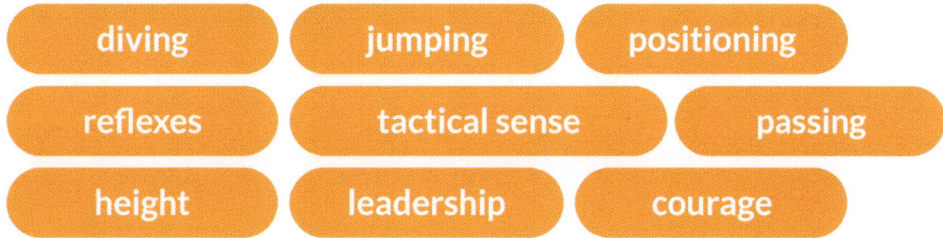

Goalkeeper out of possession

Defend the space
Effective actions to protect the area outside the 18 yard box.

Support
Connecting the team through positioning, instruction and action to best manage the goal, area and space.

Defend the area
Effective actions to protect balls played into the 18 yard box.

Defend the goal
Effective actions to prevent the goals being scored.

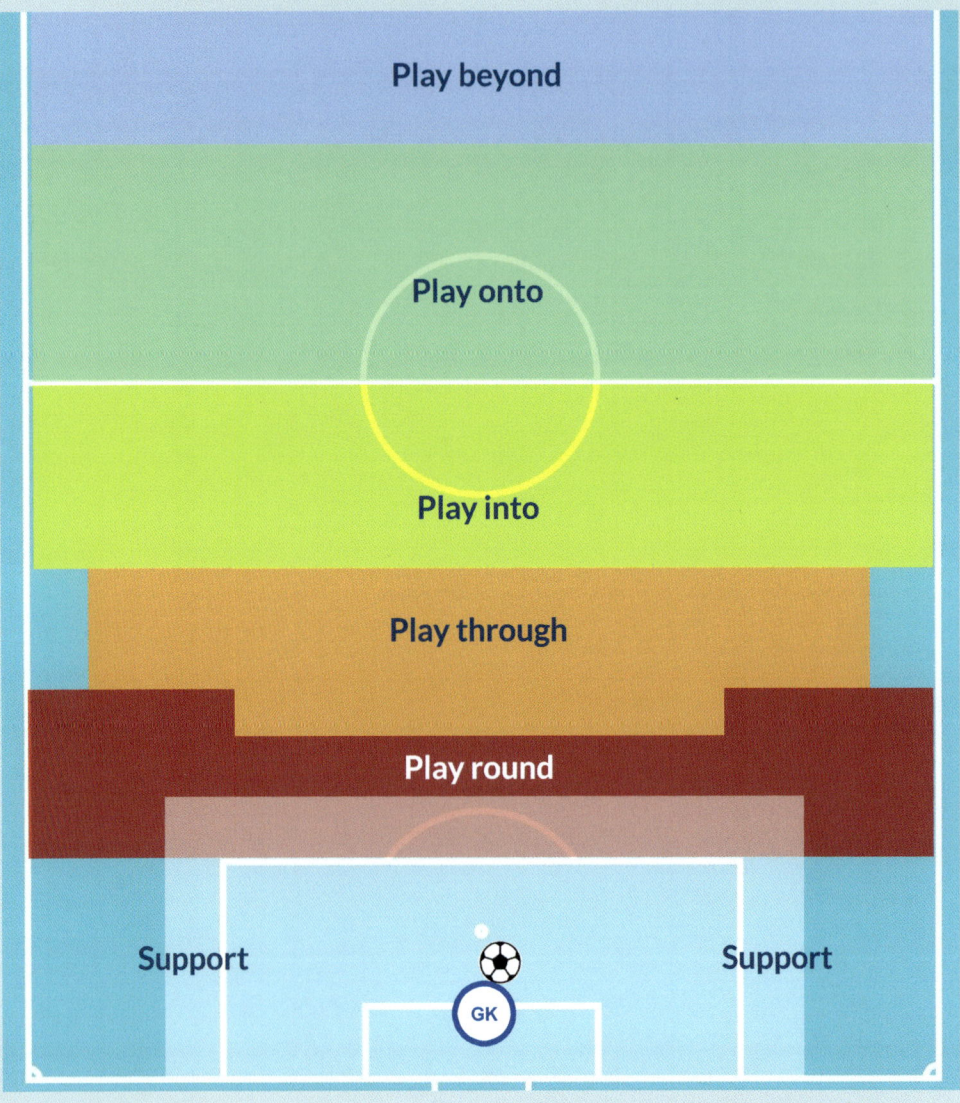

Goalkeeper in possession

Play beyond
Passing to the **space beyond** the opposition backline.

Play onto
Passing to teammates optimising the chances of winning the **aerial duel**.

Play into
Playing penetrative passes **over** opposition players.

Play through
Playing penetrative passes **between** opposition players.

Play round
Circulating the ball in preparation to penetrate the opposition.

Support
Providing the optimum **position** for the specific in-possession phase of the game.

Centre-back

Virgil Van Dijk, Netherlands

Centre-back

Centre-backs are defenders who are positioned in an area directly in front of the goal to prevent opposing players from scoring.

There are 2 types of Centre-back (CB), the **Stopper** (no. 5) and the **Sweeper** (no. 6), although in modern football players are working hard toward being able to play both roles. CB can be 2 or 3, depending on how many players are forming the defensive line: for instance, there are **3 CB** in the 3-5-2 and 3-4-3, there are **2 CB** in the 4-4-2 and 4-3-3, and again **3 CB** in the 5-3-2.

Steph Houghton, England

The **Stopper**'s main aim is to stop the Striker from scoring. They have no fear in using their body to block the ball, contesting headers and performing strong tackles on opponents.

The **Sweeper** (or Libero) is leading the defense, managing the offside line and cleaning up loose balls. They are free from marking attackers in open play, have awareness, vision and passing ability.

Central defenders strategies:
- **Man to man marking**: each defender marks a specific player.
- **Zonal Marking**: each defender covers their area, marking any forward approaching.

Kalidou Koulibaly, Senegal

Main tasks:

- Marking opponent's forwards.
- Intercepting passes.
- Blocking shots.
- Tackling.
- Keeping the defensive line.
- Starting the action, receiving the ball from the Goalkeeper and distributing it.
- Offering a safe passing option to Full-backs and Midfielders when they have pressure or cannot find space (it helps opening opponent's lines when in possession).
- Scoring headers in the opponent's box when there are corner kicks or free kicks in attack.

Attributes required:

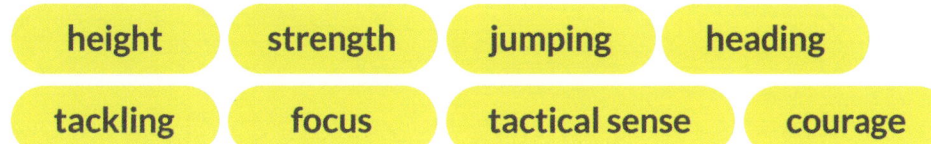

Tactical input

Principles of Football • © 2020 Enrico Pomarico

The Offside

"A player is in an offside position if any of their body parts, except the hands and arms, are in the opponent's half of the pitch, and closer to the opponent's goal line than both the ball and the second-last opponent (the last opponent is usually, but not necessarily, the goalkeeper)."

Offside is judged at the moment the ball is last touched by the most recent player, usually a pass made towards a teammate.

A player who was in an offside position at the moment the ball was last touched or played by a teammate must then become involved in active play, in the opinion of the referee, for the offence to occur.

Tactical input

Offside can be used as strategy: the defensive line, all the defenders, whether they are 3, 4 or 5 (most commonly used with a line of 4), would step forward at the same time in the moment when it seems obvious that the midfielder is about to pass the ball forward to an attacker, putting him in an offside position.

Although it may help keeping the opponent team far from the goal, **a defensive strategy based exclusively on the offside can be very dangerous** because it's enough that a player is late on following the defensive line movements or that the opponent attackers are very good at avoiding it to leave the entire defensive half open for counterattacks.

Full-backs

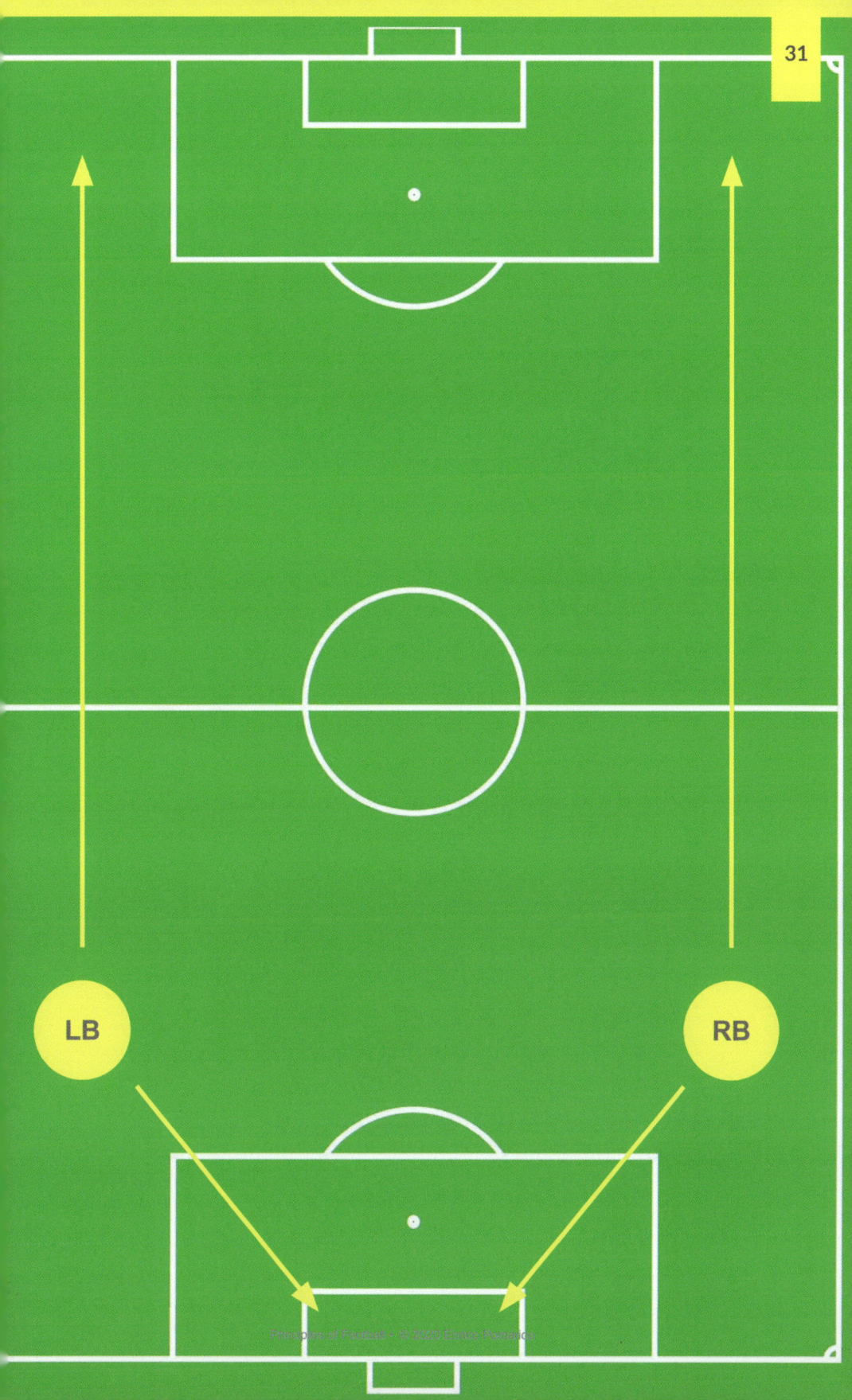

Marcelo, Brazil

Full-backs

Right back (RB) and **Left back (LB)**, also known as numbers 2 and 3, are the wide defenders at the sides of the CBs in a defensive line of 4 players (i.e. 4-4-2, 4-3-3).

Their job is to mark opponent's Wingers and take part to the offensive action in certain capacity.

Full-backs can also be playing as **Wingbacks** (LWB, RWB) in teams fielding 3 CBs (i.e. 3-5-2, 3-4-3, 5-3-2) where they will be assigned more attacking and less defending responsibilities.

Main tasks:

- Providing a physical obstruction to opposition attacking players by shepherding them towards an area where they become less dangerous (i.e. towards the center where they would be forced to use their weak foot and there will be more defenders and midfielders to help blocking the way).
- Making off-the-ball runs into spaces down the channels and supplying crosses into the opponent's box.

Dani Alves, Brazil

Alexander-Arnold, Eng.

- Providing a passing option down the flank, creating opportunities for sequences like one-two passing combinations.
- Attacking Full-backs help to pin both opposition Full-backs and Wingers deeper in their own half with aggressive attacking intent. Their presence in attack also forces the opposition to withdraw players from central midfield, which can become an advantage as it might open spaces elsewhere on the pitch.
- Taking throw-ins.
- Maintaining tactical discipline keeping up with the defensive line movements for an efficient offside strategy.
- Following all the defensive movements like the Diagonal, to always be goalside compared to their direct opponent winger.

Attributes required:

pace   stamina   marking   tackling
tactical sense   dribbling   crossing

Tactical input

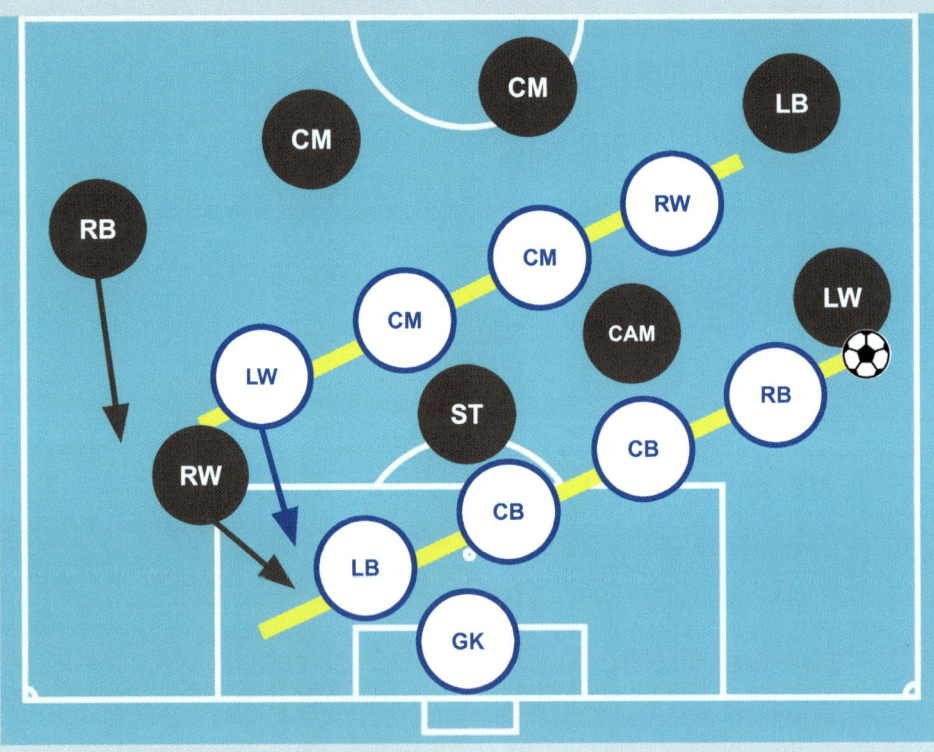

"La Diagonale"
(Diagonal Shuffling)

Diagonal shuffling is a defensive movement that applies when using zonal marking, especially with the defensive line of 4. The offside trap is mainly used when the opponent's ball carrier and the whole defensive block are operating in the center. **Once the ball moves onto one of the flanks the concept of Diagonal Shuffling steps in.** Whilst a Full-back is blocking the opponent on one side the rest of the defenders align themselves in a diagonal shape so that the other Full-back on the opposite side can defend crosses on the **second post**. At the same time, the CBs are blocking any diagonal passing or dribbling towards the inside.

Even the Midfielders have to **shuffle down** if the opponent is attacking the space with many players. Often the Wingers end up saving the team from conceding a goal by following the opponent's Full-backs all the way to the **back post**.
Once the opponents have moved the ball towards the center, the defensive line and all the defensive block return to its normal shape.

Central midfielders

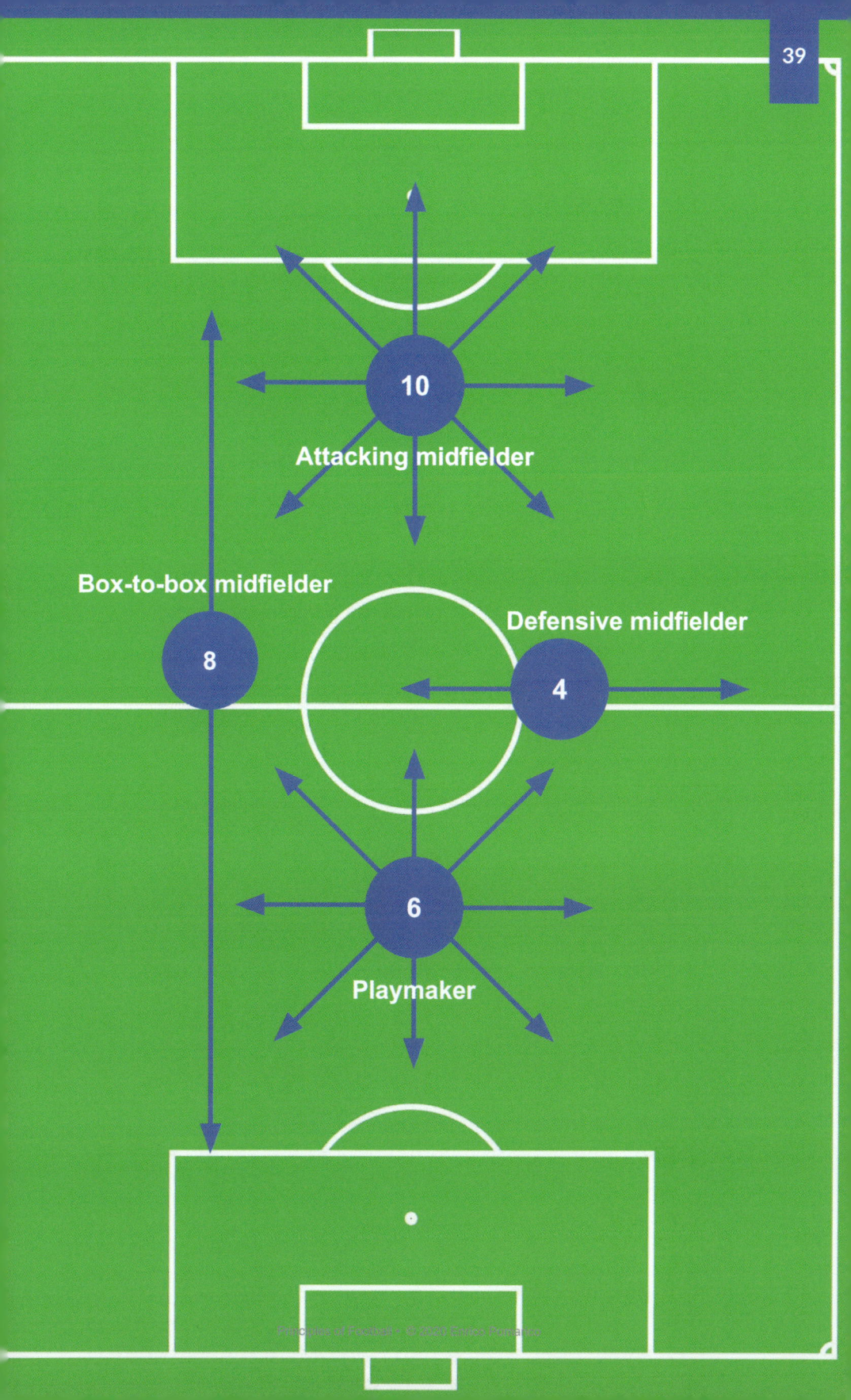

10 Attacking midfielder

8 Box-to-box midfielder

4 Defensive midfielder

6 Playmaker

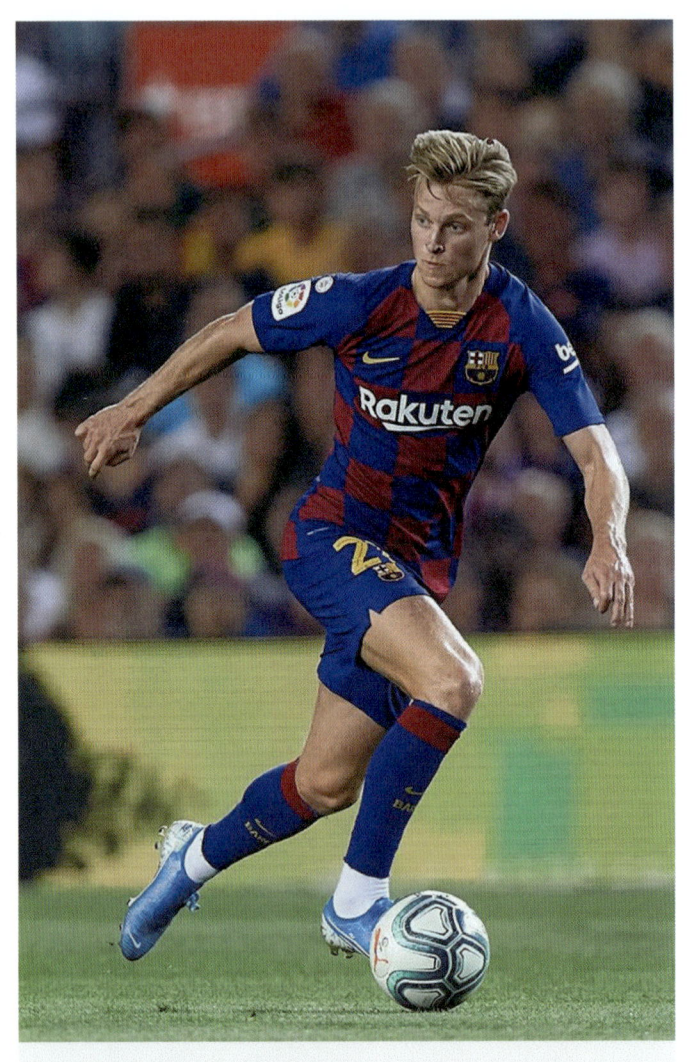

Frankie DeJong, Netherlands

Central midfielders

There are various kinds of Central midfielders as players have different physical, technical and tactical characteristics. In addition, different formations, strategies and styles of play need specific types of players.

- **Playmaker**
- **Defensive midfielder**
- **Box-to-box midfielder**
- **Attacking midfielder**

There are of course all rounded players that can cover more than one of the above positions if required, thanks to their variety of skills and characteristics.

Jorginho, Italy

Playmaker

Most teams have a Playmaker, a player who controls and dictates the tempo of the game and brings others into play. The Playmaker connects defense and midfield in the building up of the action with their amazing `passing` skills, `technique` and `tactical sense`.

Their `vision` allows them to see unexpected lines of passing to the forwards that could surprise the opposition in any moment of the match.
A Playmaker is like a coach on the pitch putting order when in possession and breaking up opponent's attacks when out of possession.
Teams with playing style based on possession and game control absolutely need a player with those characteristics.

N'Golo Kanté, France

Defensive midfielder

The Defensive midfielder (CDM, often wearing no. 4) is one of the hardest roles: they are doing a lot of obscure work that too often doesn't get the recognition it deserves.
Also known as **Holding midfielder**, they are tactically minded, often covering other player's positions when they venture forward.
In some cases Defensive midfielders may take on a deep-lying Playmaker role, where they can dictate the play with long and short passes.

Attributes required:

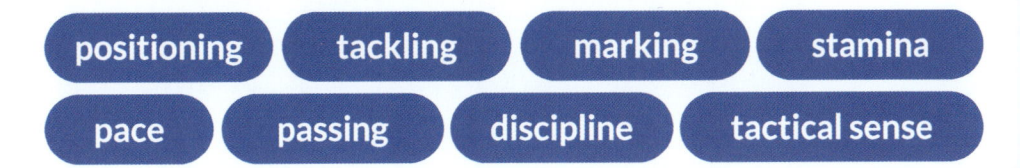

- positioning
- tackling
- marking
- stamina
- pace
- passing
- discipline
- tactical sense

Paul Pogba, France

Box-to-box midfielder

A Box-to-box midfielder, also known as **Mezzala** or number 8, is a strong all rounded CM who is capable of defending and attacking for the whole match length.

Their main characteristics, besides their amazing endurance, are overlapping runs into space and vertical dribbling penetrations. These abilities lead them to contribute with many goals and assists as they represent a consistent danger for the opponent's defense.

Attributes required:

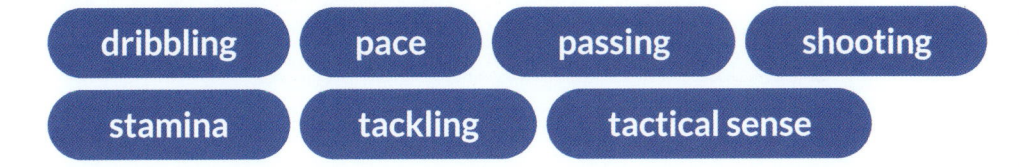

- dribbling
- pace
- passing
- shooting
- stamina
- tackling
- tactical sense

Kevin De Bruyne, Belgium

Attacking midfielder

Also known as **number 10, Fantasista or Trequartista**, the Attacking midfielder (CAM) is often the star of the team being the player with the most `technique` and advanced `leadership` skills.

Just as advanced Playmakers, they have got the ability to connect midfield and attack, working with `creativity` and unpredictability in an area of the pitch where the defense pressure and focus is at its maximum.

They would create a scoring opportunity for themselves or for a teammate thanks to their accurate `passing` and outstanding `vision`. Most of the times CAM are in charge of taking penalties, free-kicks and even corner kicks, because of their sublime `shooting` skills.

Lionel Messi, Argentina

Sometimes the no. 10 may play so close to the Striker to become an actual **Second Striker** or replace completely the Striker becoming a **False 9** (or "Falso Nueve").

A great example of this is when Messi plays Centre Forward dropping deep into midfield to find space in between the opponent's lines of defense and midfield.

No. 10s prefer to receive the ball on their back foot and facing forward, that's when they are the most unpredictable and fully unleash their talent and creativity.

A signature skill of gifted players wearing the 10 is the oriented control: directing the ball with the first touch, controlling it and moving it into space at the same time.

Tactical input

Compactness ❌

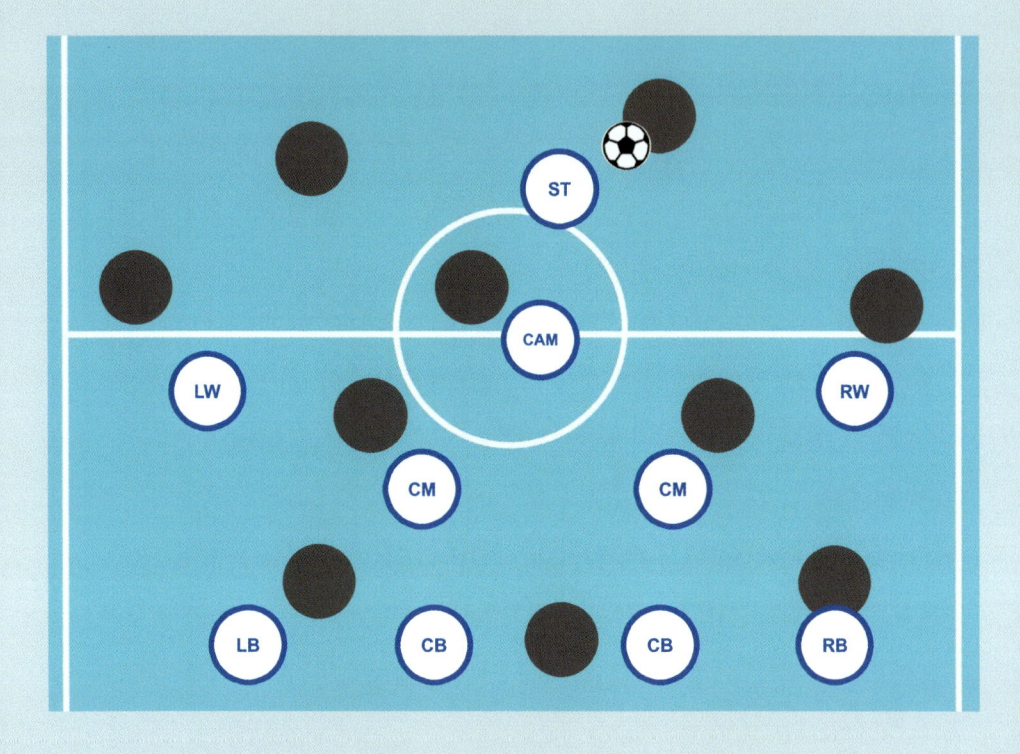

The defensive block is covering a large space with little control over it, leaving the ball carrier with many options available in comfortable spaces. The team in possession will go through the defensive line with easy 1-2 combinations and basic off-the-ball movements.

Compactness ✓

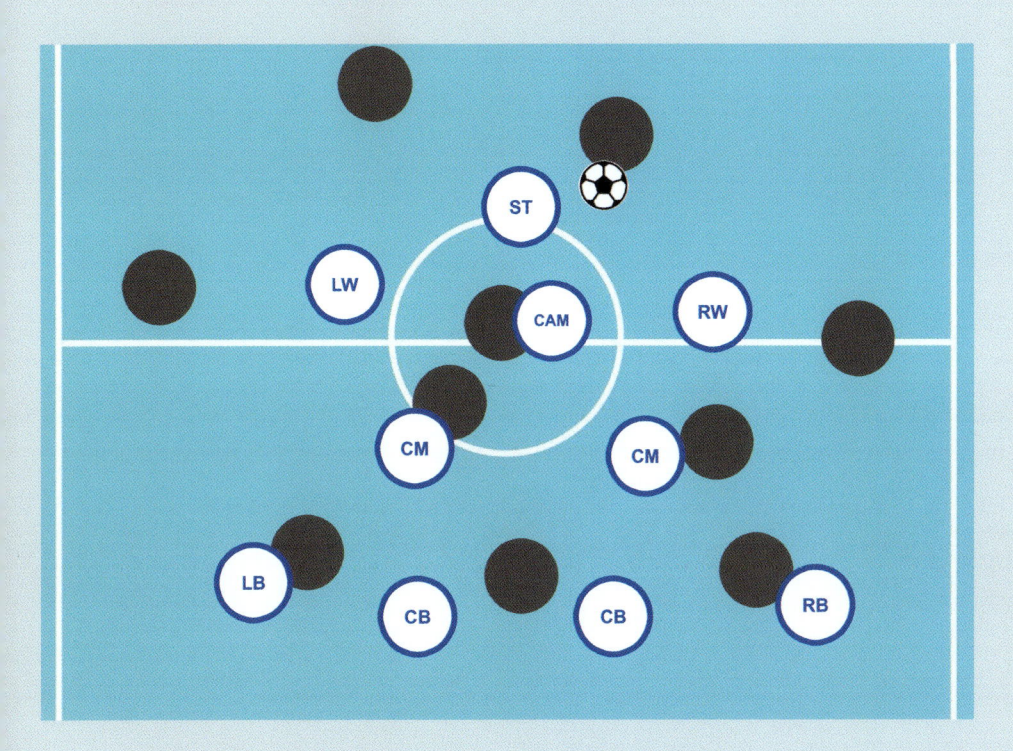

The defensive block is covering less space but exerting a large degree of **control** over it. Most lines of passing are locked as the spaces are narrow and multiple players can easily **intercept**. The block will **shuffle** on the side when the ball will be played wide on the flanks.

Wingers

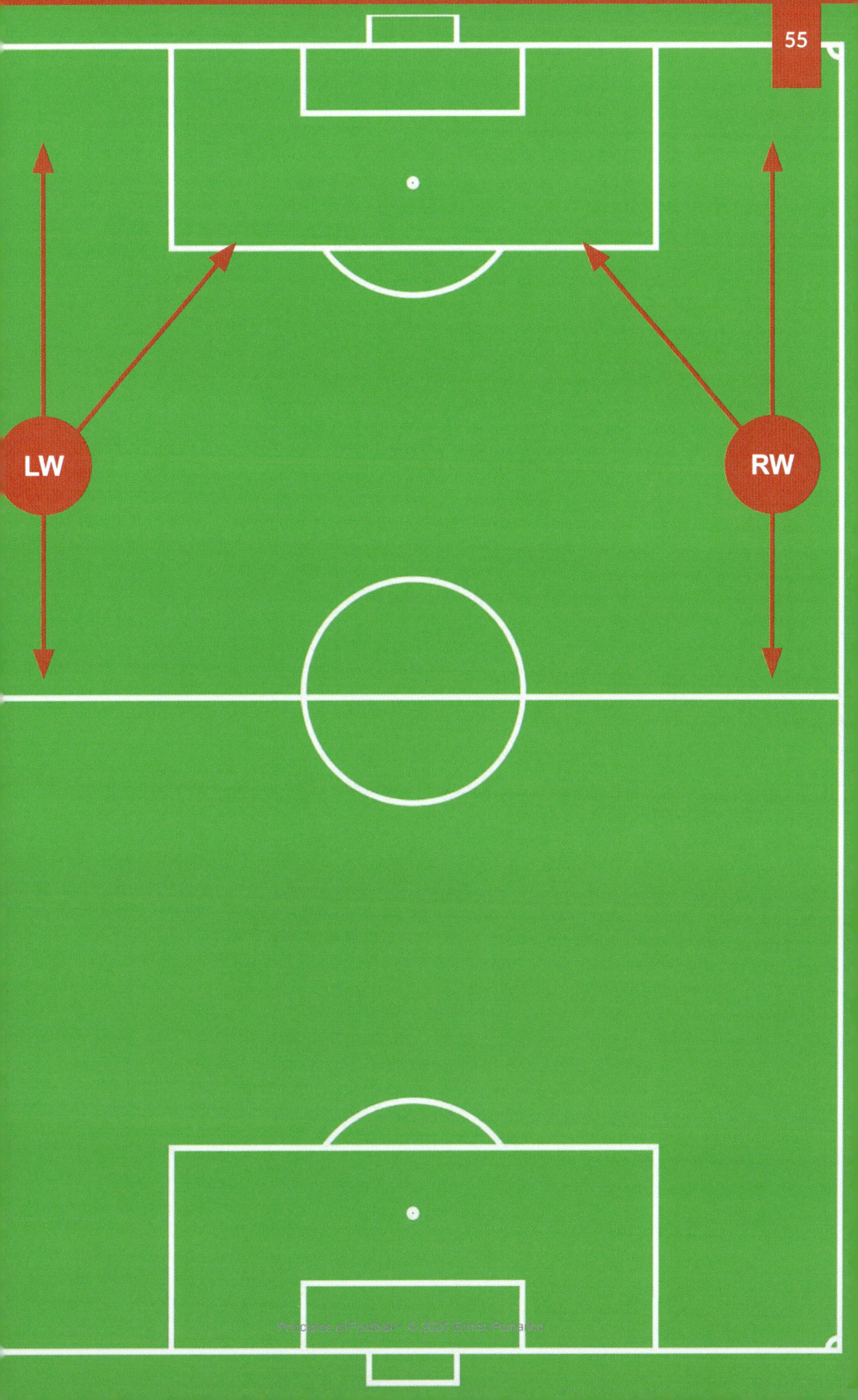
LW
RW

Ousmane Dembélé, France

Wingers

Right Winger (RW, no. 7) and **Left Winger** (LW, no. 11) are wide attacking players positioned on the respective flanks protected by the the RB and the LB.
However with the concepts of pressing and compactness they have an important involvement in the defensive phase.

In a 4-4-2 formation they would be **Right midfielder** (RM) and **Left midfielder** (LM) or in some variations of the 4-3-3 they can be called **Right forward** (RF) and **Left forward** (LF) but they are basically the same players with more or less the same tasks, only placed higher up or deeper down.
Their specialty is the 1v1 so teams that play with Wingers will try to isolate them in large wide spaces where they are most dangerous.

Toni Duggan, England

Main tasks:

- Staying close to the side line to pull wide the fullbacks.
- Cutting through the middle of the defense.
- Staying onside.
- Looking for one-two combinations.
- Making overlapping runs.
- Attacking the space.
- Challenging the direct opponent 1v1 with dribbling.
- Crossing in the box.
- Switching the ball across to the opposite side.
- Pressing high when required.
- Holding and intercepting.
- Following and marking the fullbacks all the way to their goal kick line.

Attributes required:

dribbling   pace   crossing   shooting

Tactical input

Crossing zones

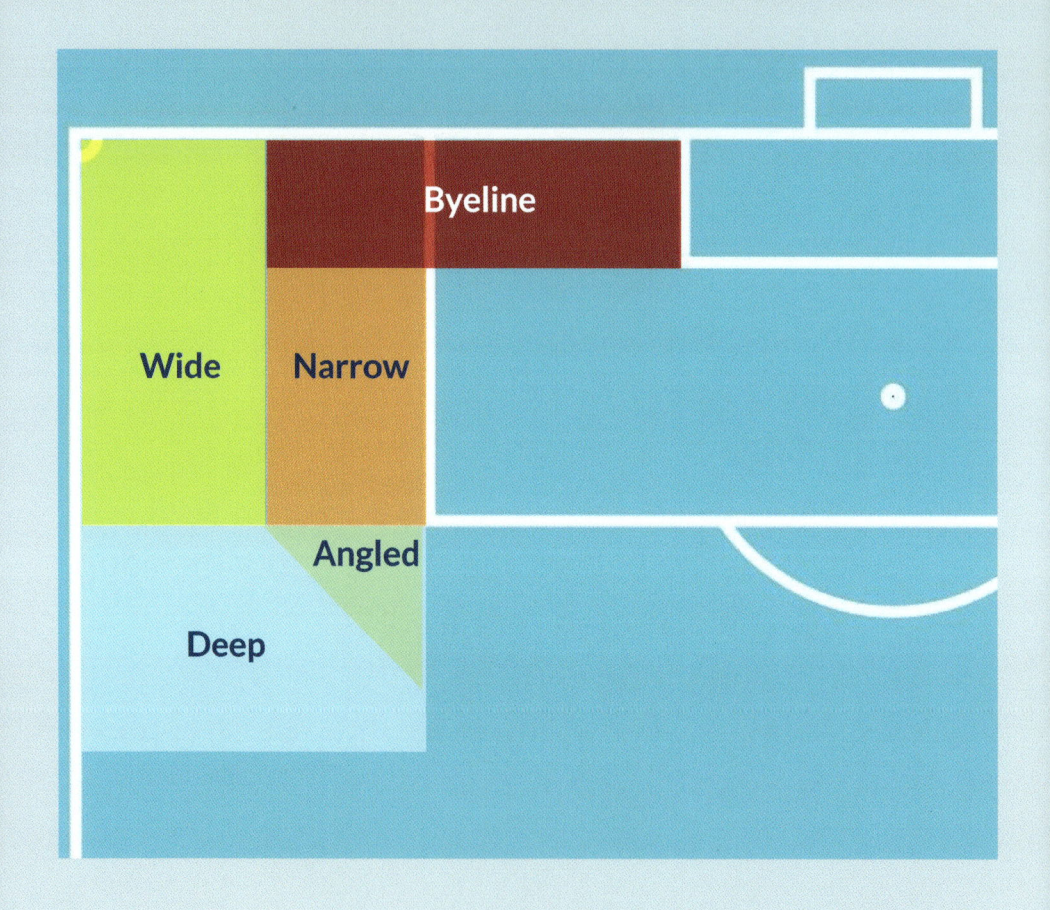

- Byeline
- Wide
- Narrow
- Angled
- Deep

Principles of Football • © 2020 Enrico Pomarico

Crossing zones

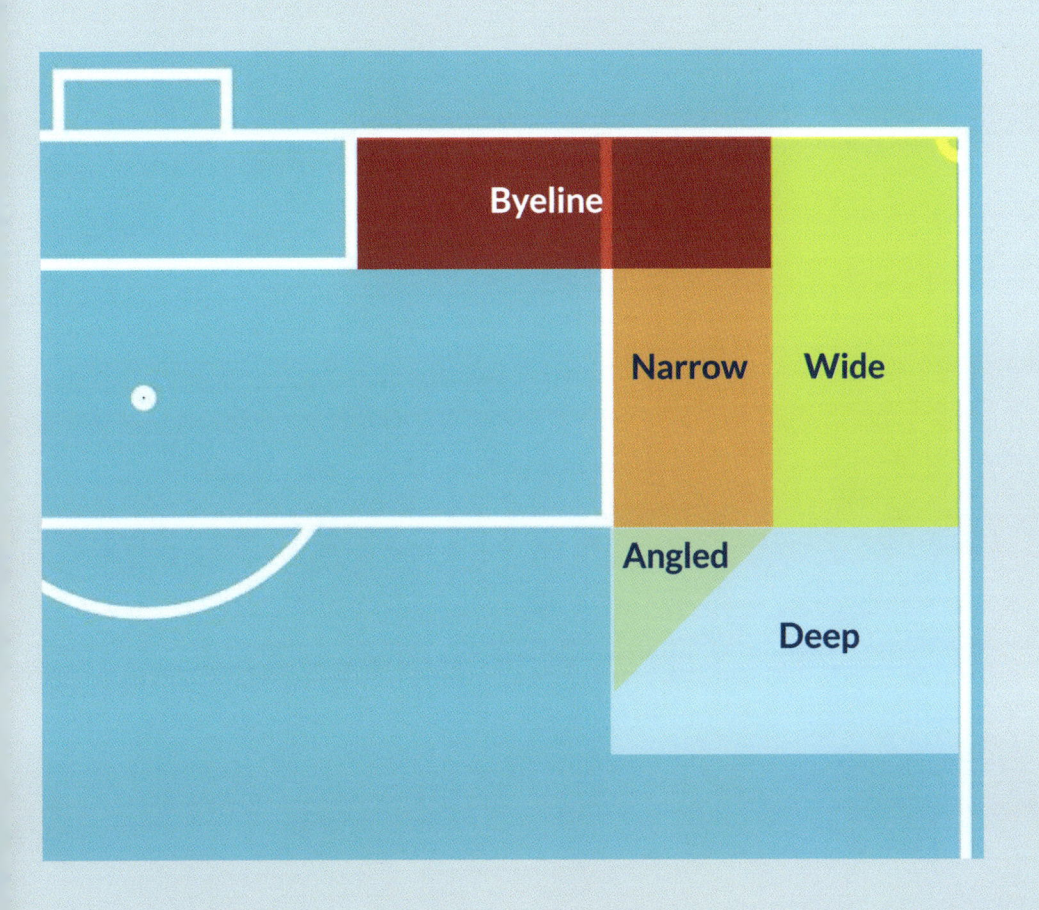

Striker

9

Striker

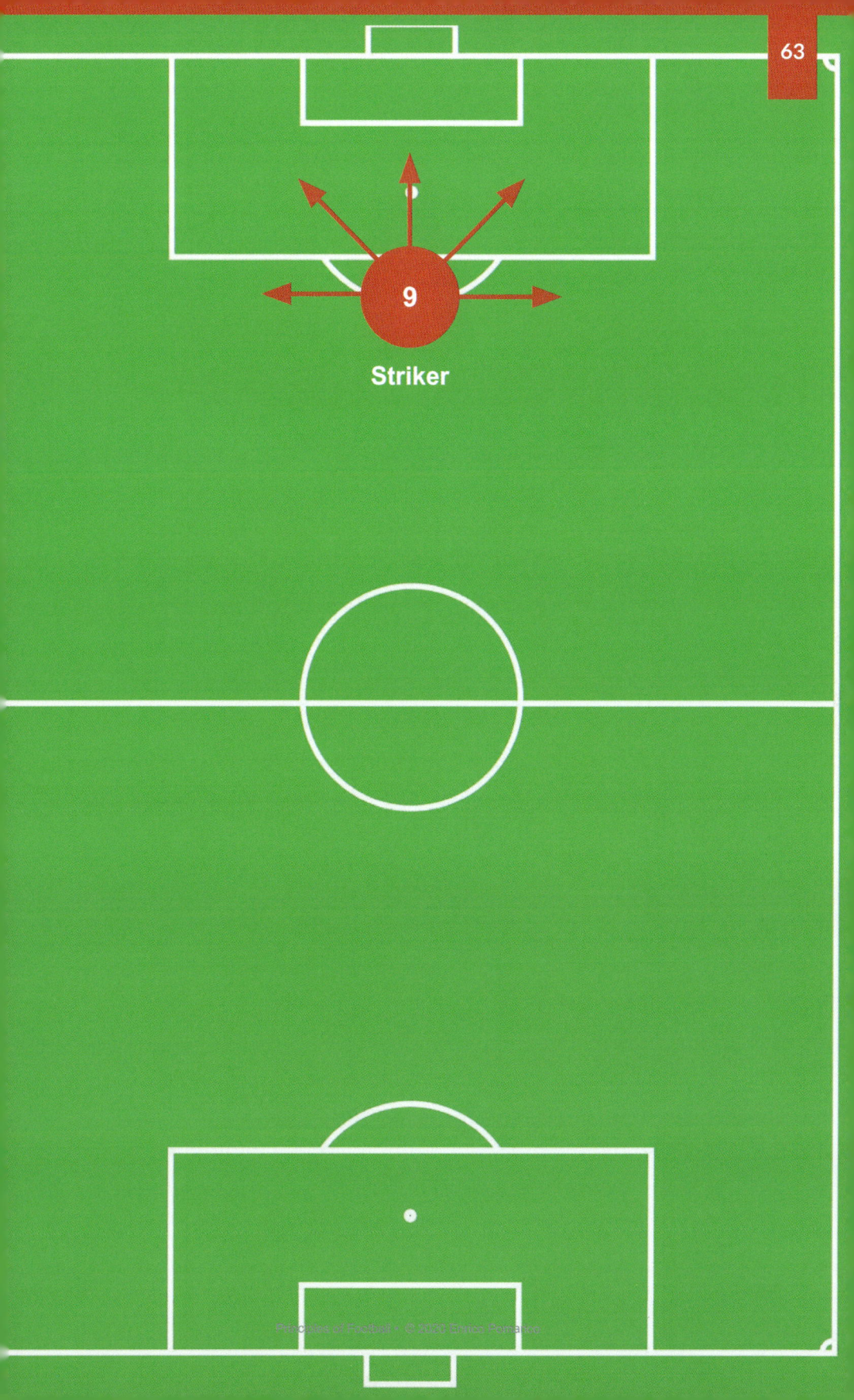

Erling Haaland, Norway

Striker

The **Striker** (ST) or **Centre Forward** (CF) is the number 9, the most advanced player of the team. Served by the number 10, the Wingers, the Midfielders and even the Full-backs, the Striker is the player supposed to score most of the goals.

The Striker is paradoxically the first defender of the team bringing very aggressive pressure high upfield.
Indeed modern football is often based on possession and opponents are starting the action from the back. Pressing is effective only if done by all the players at the same time and with the same intensity, so the ST has a crucial role in reading, coordinating and leading the first moments of the defensive phase.

Cristiano Ronaldo, Portugal

Based on physical and technical characteristics, there are at least 4 types of Strikers:

- **The Target Man**
  Strong `physicality` and `headers` specialists, they can hold the ball up to bring teammates into play. More of an assist man than a goal scorer.

- **The Finisher (or Poacher)**
  `Positioning` and goal scoring instinct. They are always roaming in and around the box with excellent movements off the ball. Very accurate `shooting`.

- **The Dribbler**
  Great `pace` and `agility` to change direction and leave a defender behind. These skills are often combined with clinical finishing.

- **The Complete Forward**
  They have got all the attributes described above!

Tactical input

Striker's tricks

Deceiving the opponent
Strikers always make 2 runs, 1 for the defender and 1 for themselves. Deception is important as it gives the player an extra yard and/or a momentum advantage on the marking opponent.

Observing the opponent
Knowing what we are up against is always an advantage. Strikers will try taking a physical defender out of his comfort zone, a slower player into wider runs, a weaker player into physical challenges and so on.

Beating the offside trap
Often we notice Strikers staying in offside position on purpose. It is unnerving for the defender not to be able to see attacking players roaming on their blind side.
The striker will quickly step back in an onside position when a teammate is ready to pass the ball through.

Moving like a snake
Bending the run is also important, running straight lines can easily get the forwards caught in an offside position.
Sudden and frequent changes of direction are also key movements to get away from man marking.

Finishing on the move
Sometimes receiving the ball on the run is not ideal as it might not come perfectly. Strikers would possibly shoot it first-time (without controlling it) as it would anticipate and surprise defenders and GKs.

Keep calm and freeze the goalkeeper
Once in the box with the ball at their feet many players would panic, let the emotions take over and miss. In 1v1 with the GK a good Striker keeps calm, observes well and places the ball where it should be. That cool approach makes the opponent completely freeze.

Manager

The Manager, also known as Boss, Gaffer, Coach, Mister, is the one in charge of the team and the person considered responsible for every victory and every defeat.

71

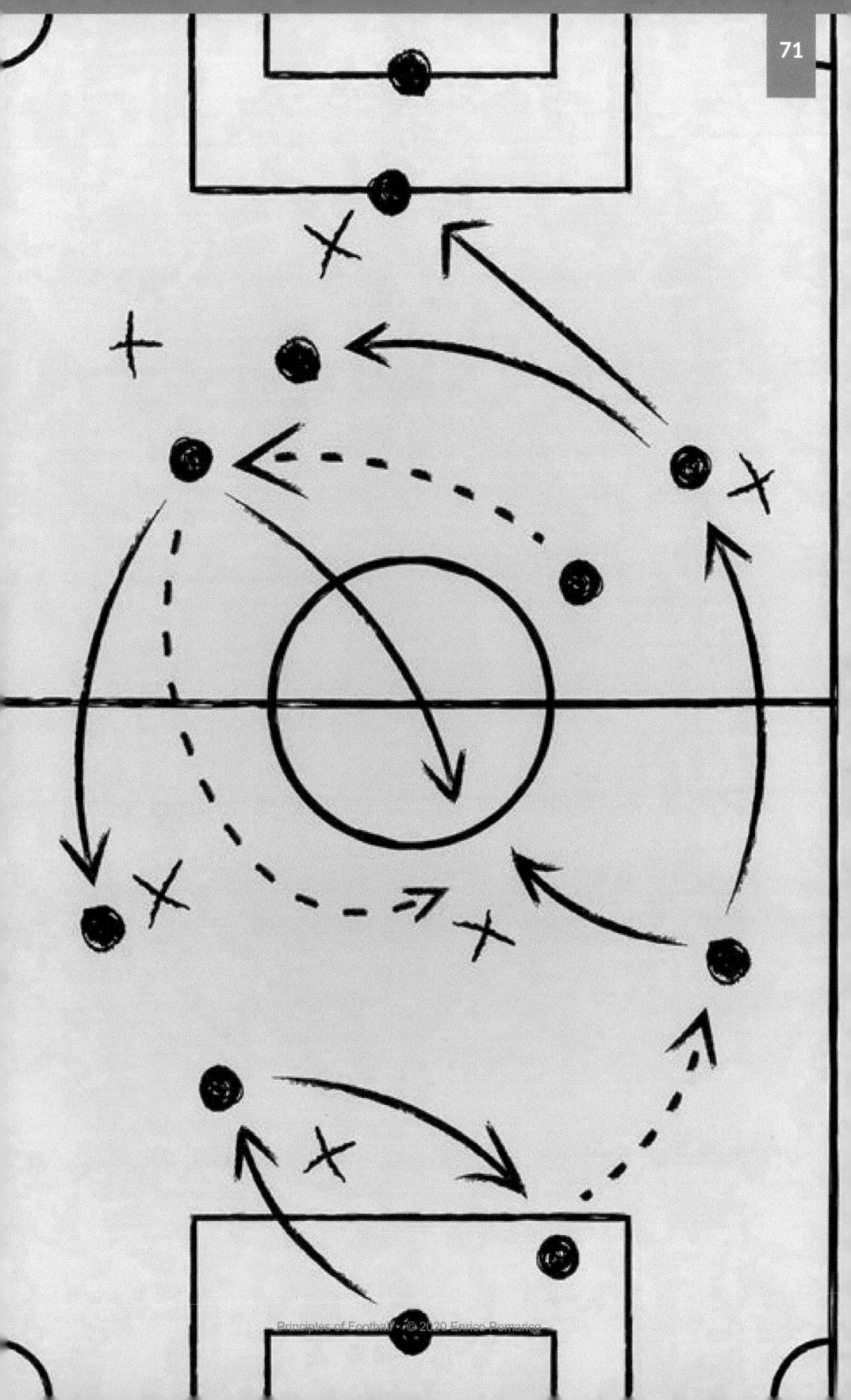

Jose Mourinho, Pt. • Pep Guardiola, Esp.

Manager

Main tasks:

- Building the team in the transfer market, signing players needed for their ideas and letting go the ones who are not necessary.
- Preparing the team for each season, physically, technically and most importantly tactically as everyone has to understand the style of play, the various strategies and to practice them together to perfection.
- Motivating players, managing relations, expectations and behaviors of the players and of the coaching and medical staff.

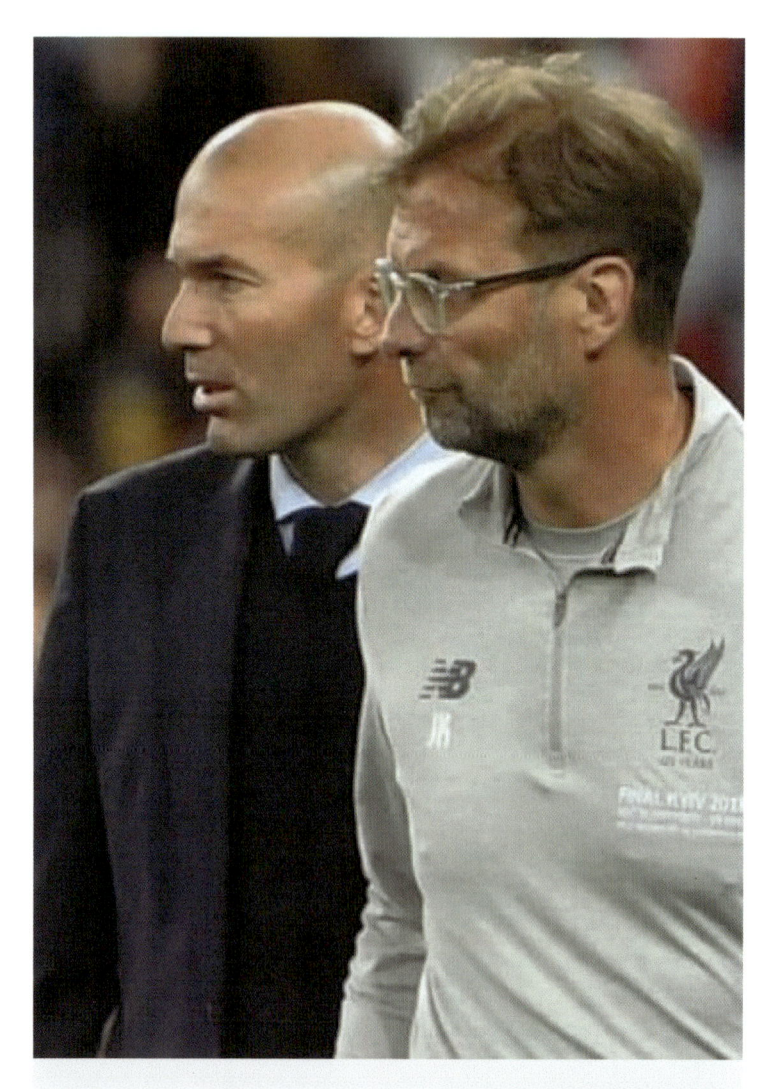

Zinedine Zidane, Fr. • **Jürgen Klopp**, De.

- Delegating duties.
- Planning the strategy for each match and instructing the team.
- Selecting the team playing each match, the formation on the pitch, the substitutes on the bench and who's out on the stands.
- Coaching the team from the sideline during matches. Directing and changing.
- Press conferences and interviews before and after the matches.
- Managers may have more or less financial and marketing responsibilities.

Tactical input

Manager's strategies

Most managers are strongly convinced of their ideas and would get the players to learn how to play their style or sign players who are already familiar with it.
Some others learn about the players and enjoy creating strategies around the already existing style, working with the players's characteristics.
A good manager also changes players, formations and strategies during the match depending on the score, the state of the game and several other factors.

Managers use one or more of the following strategies:
- **Man-to-man vs Zonal**
- **Holding deep & Counterattack**
- **Keeping possession**
- **Pressing high**

Tactical input

Man-to-man vs Zonal

Man-to-man means that each player is man marking an assigned opponent player, whilst with **Zonal** marking each player is assigned an area to cover. **Zonal** also involves **Offside** trap and the **Diagonal** movement, a lot more tactic and theory for players to study and practice, whilst **Man-to-man** is more physical and easier to execute.

The difference between the two is more visible on set pieces (corner kicks and free kicks). Which system is the best remains an everlasting dispute!

Holding deep & Counterattack

Typical of very physical teams, **Holding deep & Counterattack** is a strategy that requires a lot of patience, attention, communication and hard work. The whole team (or almost all) is behind the line of the ball. They lay deep and narrow down all possible lines of passing, checking the shoulders to keep an eye on blind sides. **Compactness** is key.

When the opponent reaches the halfway line (in some cases even deeper) the holding players apply more pressure and increasingly as the opponent advances. Once gained possession, the team needs a player with good passing skills, vision and rapidity of execution plus, of course, another player with great pace and good finishing skills if possible.

This strategy is often used to face stronger teams, where not conceding goals is the priority.

Keeping possession

Opponents can't score if they don't have the ball. A concept so true yet so hard to apply. Nowadays the top teams possess such an array of top players that leaves them with 1 ultimate mission: dominating the game. Comfortable with their skills they will make the ball (and the opponents) go around playing on two touches and with clever off-the-ball movements. With this style, commonly known as **Tiki-Taka,** they will find the way to get through opponent's lines and scoring lots of goals.
If the opponent is increasing the pressure, the team in possession will increase the tempo and play wider in order to open up the tight defending and to achieve the same results.

Pressing high

Pressing high upfield is perhaps the most demanding strategy in terms of consuming energy, keeping focused and taking risks. Pressing is effective only if done collectively so it requires planning, dedication, sacrifice and a lot of communication.
The purpose of **Pressing high** is to gain possession in the final third.
The risk of **Pressing High** is to leave many players behind and the defense uncovered when the opponent team manages to get past the pressure.

Tactical input

Technical language

Boot it
(for the GK)
to launch the
ball far and high

Drop
go back in
defense

Clear
clear the area
from the danger
by kicking the ball
away

Up
move forward
to bring up
the defensive
line

Line
pass it along
the line or
block the pass
along the line

One-Two
pass and move
into space
to receive the ball
back

**Keep it /
Keep ball**
keep the
possession within
your own team

First & Second
encouragement to
win air ball battles
(first) or to gain
the rebound
(second ball)

Switch
pass the ball
across the pitch
from one side to
the other

Drive
keep going with
the ball
at your feet

Cut
make a sprint
movement
to cut through
the opponent's
defensive line

Sources:

- *The FA Education*
- *Fifa.com*
- *Wikipedia*

Acknowledgements

Dedicated to all the players of Jolof Sports FC, from the U5 to the first team, who inspired me to write during the Covid-19 lockdown in Spring 2020.

Also special thanks to
My son Ciro-Mael who stimulates me everyday with his passion for football.
Sandrine Herbert-Razafinjato for the precious design & layout work.
Ahmadou Seye who gave me the opportunity to become a coach and the head coach of our youth teams, and to gain so much experience in the past 8 years.
Dan Brissett and Giovanni Cerra for contributing to verify the content and Shaun Spencer for helping out with the correct wording.
Melchiorre Infranca, the best coach I've ever had.
My parents Anna and Ciro who taught me the importance of culture.

Principles of Football

by coach Enrico Pomarico

ISBN: 9798646517211
Independently published • © 2020

Printed in Great Britain
by Amazon